Sea Rhythms
A Kid's Guide To Cabo San Lucas

Photography by John D. Weigand
Poetry by Penelope Dyan

Bellissima Publishing, LLC
Jamul, California
www.bellissimapublishing.com

Copyright © 2017 by Penny D. Weigand and John D. Weigand

All rights reserved. No part of this book may be
reproduced or transmitted in any form or by any means,
electronic or mechanical, including photocopying,
recording, or by any other means, or by any information or
storage retrieval system, without permission from the publisher.

ISBN 978-1-61477-272-9
First Edition

"To me the sea is a continual miracle; The fishes that swim, the rocks, the motion of the waves, the ships with men in them. What stranger miracles are there?"

Walt Whitman

Sea Rhythms
Bellissima Publishing, LLC

Introduction

Cabo San Lucas, is commonly called Cabo and is a city at the southern tip of the Baja California Peninsula, in the Mexican state of Baja California Sur. Cabo San Lucas together with San José del Cabo is known as Los Cabos, and it is a great vacation destination with a lot of things to see and do! You can go to the beach, surf or go fishing, scuba or snorkel, and go shopping! Cabo is enjoyed by everyone, natives of Mexico and tourists alike,

Written by award winning author, attorney and former teacher, Penelope Dyan, and complemented by the beautiful photographs of John D. Weigand, this book is perfect for kids! Its size is easy to handle, and its large print is perfect for young eyes. It is easy to fit this book into a kid-sized backpack, and it can be used in conjunction with practicing reading skills, because of the author's careful use of word repetition, word recognition and rhyme. Most of all, this book is meant for kids, and it is meant to show a kid the things a kid will notice when he or she travels! And to make the learning experience even more fun, there is a free music video kids can watch on the Bellissimavideo YouTube channel that goes with this book!

Sea Rhythms
Bellissima Publishing, LLC

Sea Rhythms
A Kid's Guide To Cabo San Lucas

Photography by John D. Weigand
Poetry by Penelope Dyan

There is a rhythm to the sea,
felt by every fish, bird and bee.

And to its harbors and ports
we are inexplicably drawn,
as if by the mermaids' siren song.

Its waves can be quiet
or they can pound against the shore.
You never really know what for YOU,
the ocean has in store.

You can play in its waters.
or you can relax on its soft sand,
if you choose NOT to be sea bound,
and instead remain upon the land.

And if you wish,
you can go fishing,
and you might catch a BIG fish!

And, of course, there is more!
You can go shopping near the shore!

And when you head out
into the ocean blue,
adventure will lie ahead for you.

Your boat will dock at some rocks,
on an island's sandy shore.
And you can get out of the boat,
if you want to explore!

There is a sea cave you see
(from the boat.)
But you do not stop and go inside,
even though to YOU
it looks like a GREAT place to hide!
And if you were a pirate,
it would be your pleasure
to hide deep INSIDE that cave,
with ALL your pirate treasure!

Your mom sees these sea lions
resting upon the rocks.
And she looks at dad and says,
"At least THEY don't have CLOCKS!"
And your dad smiles as he listens
to what SHE has just said,
and he knows mom would have rather
simply stayed ALL day in bed!

You see another rock in the sea.
And you can't HELP wondering why
it looks just like a stone elephant,
reaching right up to the sky!

You see a lovers' beach,
secluded in the sea.
And Mom says this beach
is a lovely place to be.
And this is a clue that dad
just can't miss,
as he reaches over
to give Mom a kiss!
The rhythm of the seas,
has touched Dad's heart,
and from this place,
you will soon sadly depart.
You think, "Tomorrow is another day,"
as from this beach you drift away.

"Our memories of the ocean will linger on, long after our footprints in the sand are gone."

Unknown Author

www.ingramcontent.com/pod-product-compliance
Ingram Content Group UK Ltd.
Pitfield, Milton Keynes, MK11 3LW, UK
UKHW060134240426
12048UKWH00002B/38